BIRMINGHAM
REPERTORY
THEATRE

**Birmingham Repertory Theatre,
Hull Truck Theatre and Watford Palace Theatre present**

FOLK

by Tom Wells

Folk premiered in The STUDIO at
Birmingham Repertory Theatre on 14 April 2016

FOLK

by Tom Wells

CAST

Stephen   **Patrick Bridgman**
Kayleigh   **Chloe Harris**
Winnie   **Connie Walker**

CREATIVES

Director   **Tessa Walker**
Designer   **Bob Bailey**
Lighting Designer   **Simon Bond**
Composer and Musical Director   **James Frewer**
Sound Designer   **Clive Meldrum**
Assistant Director   **Jo Gleave**
Recipient of a JMK Regional
Assistant Director Bursary

JMK trust | in memory of James Menzies-Kitchin

Stage Manager   **Michael Ramsay**
Deputy Stage Manager   **Amber Curtis**

Supported by

THE SIR BARRY JACKSON TRUST

Supported using public funding by
ARTS COUNCIL ENGLAND

This production and the UK tour are supported
by the Sir Barry Jackson Trust.

Birmingham City Council

Hull City Council

WATFORD BOROUGH COUNCIL

BIRMINGHAM REPERTORY THEATRE

About Birmingham Repertory Theatre

Birmingham Repertory Theatre Company is one of Britain's leading producing theatre companies. Founded in 1913 by Sir Barry Jackson, Birmingham Repertory Theatre Company rapidly became one of the most famous and exciting theatre companies in the country launching the careers of an array of many great British actors including Laurence Olivier, Ralph Richardson, Edith Evans, Paul Scofield, Derek Jacobi, Elizabeth Spriggs, Albert Finney and many more.

The REP's aim is to inspire a lifelong love of theatre in the diverse communities of Birmingham and beyond. As well as presenting over 60 productions on its three stages every year, the theatre tours its productions nationally and internationally, showcasing theatre made in Birmingham. The commissioning and production of new work lies at the core of The REP's programme and over the last 15 years the company has produced more than 130 new plays. The theatre's outreach programme is the best of any cultural organisation in the city and engages with over 7000 young people and adults through its learning and participation programme equating to 30,000 individual educational sessions.

The REP is also committed to nurturing new talent through its youth theatre groups and training for up-and-coming writers, directors and artists through its REP Foundry initiative. Many of The REP's productions go on to have lives beyond Birmingham, transferring to the West End and touring nationally and internationally.

Recent transfers and tours include *Of Mice and Men* (2016 UK tour), *Anita and Me* (Theatre Royal Stratford East), *Back Down* (UK tour), *The King's Speech* (national tour), *Rudy's Rare Records* (Hackney Empire), *Khandan (Family)* (Royal Court), *Twelve Angry Men* (West End), Philip Pullman's *I Was a Rat!* (national tour) and Kate Tempest's *Hopelessly Devoted* (national tour).

The REP's long-running production of *The Snowman* celebrated its 21st anniversary in 2014. It has become a must-see fixture in London's West End calendar, playing to packed houses at the Peacock Theatre every Christmas for a record-breaking 18 years. *The Snowman* also tours regularly across the UK and to theatres in Holland, Korea, Japan and Finland.

www.birmingham-rep.co.uk

BIRMINGHAM REPERTORY THEATRE

About Hull Truck Theatre

Hull Truck Theatre is a creative community of people dedicated to delivering exceptional theatre for a diverse audience, including those encountering it for the first time.

We work with partners, audiences, and communities to create a vibrant cultural home, offering a diverse programme from home-grown productions to inspirational visiting work by leading UK artists. A key player in the successful bid team that delivered Hull UK City of Culture 2017, we are an ambassador for our city and a flagship for our region.

We see culture as a powerful regenerative tool for our city, enabling it to meet its ambitions and commitment to overcoming social and economic challenges. We are a pioneering theatre with a contemporary Northern Voice, locally rooted and national in reach, inspiring artists, exciting audiences and supporting communities to reach their greatest potential.

Through our work with schools and with the community, we help to raise aspirations and give life-changing creative opportunities to thousands of young people, disabled groups and adults.

'We believe that everyone has the right to enjoy and be enriched by high-quality artistic work that is culturally relevant to people and place, in a positive and welcoming environment. We aim to be a thriving creative organisation that tells extraordinary human stories, offering fresh and imaginative perspectives on the world.'

Mark Babych, Artistic Director

www.hulltruck.co.uk

HULL TRUCK THEATRE

Hull Truck Theatre gratefully acknowledges our front of house volunteer team.

Watford Palace Theatre

About Watford Palace Theatre

Watford Palace Theatre is a 21st-century producing theatre, making new work across the art forms of theatre, dance, outdoor arts and digital, and developing audiences, artists and communities through exciting opportunities to participate.

Watford Palace Theatre commissions and produces plays from a range of new and established writers. Recent premieres include: *Poppy + George* by Diane Samuels; *Coming Up* by Neil D'Souza; *Jefferson's Garden* by Timberlake Wertenbaker; *Love Me Do* by Laurence Marks and Maurice Gran; *An Intervention* by Mike Bartlett (in co-production with Paines Plough); *Shiver* by Daniel Kanaber; the Ideal World season of three new plays – *Perfect Match* by Gary Owen, *Virgin* by E.V.Crowe (in co-production with nabokov), *Override* by Stacey Gregg; *Jumpers for Goalposts* by Tom Wells (in co-production with Paines Plough and Hull Truck Theatre); *Our Brother David* by Anthony Clark; *Our Father* by Charlotte Keatley; and *Family Business* by Julian Mitchell.

Creative Associates are central to Watford Palace Theatre's vision, these include Resident Companies Rifco Arts and Tiata Fahodzi; Mahogany Opera Group: Scamp Theatre; Kate Flatt; Shona Morris; Charlotte Keatley; Gary Owen; Alice Birch and Timberlake Wertenbaker.

www.watfordpalacetheatre.co.uk

FOLK

Tom Wells

*This one's for you, Tessa Walker,
with love.*

Characters

KAYLEIGH, *fifteen*
STEPHEN, *fifties*
SISTER WINNIE, *a nun, Irish, fifties*

This text went to press before the end of rehearsals and so may differ slightly from the play as performed.

1.

SISTER WINNIE's *front room.*

WINNIE *lives in an old Victorian terraced house on Bannister Street, Withernsea.*

It's decorated simply, clean and warm and a bit shabby, with a big bay window, some religious pictures, a few lamps, a sofa and a chair. There's a staircase coming down into the room, a door through to the kitchen, and a door at the back to a yard where WINNIE *goes to smoke. Sometimes. She sometimes just smokes out of the window.*

Friday night.

STEPHEN *sits. He's got an old Aldi bag at his feet, full of handwritten music and tin whistles. Some of the tin whistles are home-made. He is holding a very battered guitar, tuning it, listening to the strings.*

WINNIE *sticks her head out from the kitchen, grinning.*

WINNIE. Cheer me up, Stephen. Sing something.

STEPHEN. Something, um, holy or…?

    WINNIE *nods.*

WINNIE. Something wholly inappropriate.

    WINNIE *disappears again.*

    STEPHEN *smiles and starts to play.* 'The Holy Ground'.

    He is all fingers and thumbs, but he bashes it out alright, and sings, quietly:

STEPHEN.
    Adieu to you my Dinah
    Ten thousand times adieu
    For we're going away from the Holy Ground
    And the girls that we love true.
    We will sail the salt seas over

And then return for shore
To see again the girls we love
And the Holy Ground once more –

WINNIE *dances in.*

WINNIE. FINE GIRL YOU ARE!

WINNIE *has two pints of Guinness. She puts the glasses down on a little table. She is jiggling along to the music.*

STEPHEN.
You're the girl I do adore
And still I live in hopes to see
The Holy Ground once more.

STEPHEN *stops singing, but carries on strumming his guitar.*

Less holy than I thought. Sorry.

WINNIE. Spot on. Just the ticket.

WINNIE *takes the second verse herself.*

And now the storm is raging
And we are far from shore
And the good old ship is tossing about
And the rigging is all tore

WINNIE *picks up a statue of the Virgin Mary, and sings to it.*

And the secret of my life, my dear,
You're the girl I do adore

She uses it as a microphone.

But still I live in hope to see
The Holy Ground once more.

STEPHEN *and* WINNIE.
FINE GIRL YOU ARE!

WINNIE.
You're the girl I do adore
But still I live in hope to see
The Holy Ground once more

A moment.

Oh. Ah.

STEPHEN. And now…

> WINNIE *pulls a face at* STEPHEN. *She has forgotten the words.* STEPHEN *starts the next verse himself.*

> And now the storm is over
> And we are safe and well
> We'll go into a public house –

> WINNIE*'s remembered the words.*

STEPHEN *and* WINNIE.
> And we'll sit and drink like hell!

STEPHEN.
> We will drink strong ale and porter

STEPHEN *and* WINNIE.
> And make the rafters roar
> And when our money is all spent
> We'll go to sea once more
> FINE GIRL –

> *A lump of muddy brick crashes through the window. Glass goes everywhere.* STEPHEN *stops playing.*

WINNIE. Shitting hell! Are you alright?

STEPHEN. Fine, I think. Are you?

> WINNIE *has opened the door.*

WINNIE. Who's there? Who was that? You there, you! Stop, please. Did you see anything? You must've. Well, someone's just lobbed a filthy great bastarding brick through… Hang on. Show me your hands. Would you mind, I mean. Listen, we can call the police now, you can get in all sorts of trouble, seven shades of, or you can come in here where it's light, I can see your hands.

> *A moment.* WINNIE *is quieter.*

Come in here, poppet. Come on now.

> WINNIE *holds the door open. She's calm again.*

> KAYLEIGH *peeps through the doorway.*

It's Kayleigh, isn't it? Is it? I used to do you an assembly on a Thursday, in juniors. Sister Winnie. Probably don't remember – you've grown, I've shrunk.

KAYLEIGH *comes in.*

This is Stephen, he won't bite.

STEPHEN *nods hello. He's not keen.*

Now then. Hold these out a sec.

WINNIE *looks at* KAYLEIGH*'s hands. She also picks up the muddy brick. The same mud is on both.*

She looks at KAYLEIGH.

KAYLEIGH. I'm properly, properly sorry.

WINNIE. It's a good start, Kayleigh. It's a good start.

KAYLEIGH. Dunno what I was thinking.

WINNIE. I hope to goodness you do know what you were thinking, Kayleigh. It's a bit of a big thing to have done if you didn't know what you were thinking.

KAYLEIGH. I mean, I wasn't aiming for you. Is what I mean.

WINNIE. I should hope not.

KAYLEIGH (*quietly*). Well I wasn't.

WINNIE. You missed, anyway. Phew. Thank you, St Scholastica, the patron saint of nuns. Or possibly St Spyridon who could be said to be the patron saint of bricks, at a push, which I for one would say this is.

A push, I mean – it's definitely a brick.

WINNIE *smiles.* KAYLEIGH *looks down.*

Now: would you mind filling me in a bit, what's going on?

KAYLEIGH *shrugs.*

Come on, Kayleigh. Why are you chucking bricks at us for?

KAYLEIGH. Not at you.

WINNIE. Chucking bricks then. In general. Not at us.

Silence.

I tell you what: you just have a think, I'll fish the shards of window out of Stephen's Guinness.

WINNIE *sits down, peers into the Guinness.*

KAYLEIGH. Did you ring the police?

WINNIE. I didn't, Kayleigh.

KAYLEIGH. Really though?

WINNIE *offers* KAYLEIGH *her phone.*

WINNIE. Check if you like – call history. I'm fairly sure it's Npower, the Bish, and a very unhelpful young man at Domino's Pizza.

KAYLEIGH. They won't deliver, not round here.

WINNIE. I know, it's outrageous.

KAYLEIGH *smiles a tiny smile.*

What?

KAYLEIGH. Your phone's old.

WINNIE. You look after it a bit, eh? Then we definitely can't be snitching on you.

STEPHEN. Sister.

WINNIE. What?

STEPHEN *looks horrified that* WINNIE *is giving* KAYLEIGH *her phone.* WINNIE*'s not fussed.*

KAYLEIGH. What about…?

KAYLEIGH *gestures towards* STEPHEN.

WINNIE. Stephen's not got a mobile. He's anti-technology.

STEPHEN. I've got a radio.

WINNIE. Exactly.

Oh.

WINNIE *fishes a big sharp chunk of glass out of the Guinness. She looks at* STEPHEN.

STEPHEN*'s annoyed.*

STEPHEN. Fresh start?

WINNIE *nods.*

WINNIE. That was the last of the Guinness, sadly. Sorry. But there's tea in the cupboard and milk in the fridge and I reckon we could all do with a couple of sugars, for the shock. Kayleigh, you up for a tea?

KAYLEIGH. Um.

WINNIE. Three teas then, Stephen, if you don't mind.

STEPHEN *goes through to the kitchen.*

There. Now we've got rid of Stephen for a minute, hogging the conversation, as per, do you want to tell me what brings you to this end of Bannister Street of a Friday night? Is it your love of the bus depot?

KAYLEIGH *shakes her head.*

Are you sure now? It's a lovely bus depot.

KAYLEIGH. Positive.

KAYLEIGH *smiles. She's sad though.*

WINNIE. If something's the matter, Kayleigh, you can tell me. That's what nuns are for.

WINNIE *considers this.*

Also, comedy.

KAYLEIGH. I didn't just come here.

WINNIE. Oh.

KAYLEIGH. Been here ages.

WINNIE. Ages doing…?

KAYLEIGH. Nothing. Nowt. Watching.

WINNIE. Watching…?

KAYLEIGH *shrugs*.

KAYLEIGH. You.

WINNIE *giggles*.

WINNIE. Spooky.

KAYLEIGH. Not like that.

Spose, I came here to see, next door. Watch them, cos they were… Watched them like bring him in and that, to church. This morning.

WINNIE. Oh.

KAYLEIGH. Then just sort of, carried on.

WINNIE. You've been out there the whole day?

KAYLEIGH *nods*.

Whereabouts?

KAYLEIGH. Just, there's like an alley.

WINNIE. Aren't you freezing?

KAYLEIGH. Got a decent coat.

WINNIE. Here, sit here.

WINNIE *puts a chair by the radiator*.

Have you eaten anything?

KAYLEIGH. Not hungry. Just wanted to, yeah. See. Say bye.

WINNIE. Poppet.

You knew him then, knew Jason?

KAYLEIGH *shrugs*.

KAYLEIGH. Sort of.

WINNIE. I don't remember seeing you at the service.

KAYLEIGH. Just stood outside. Everyone else came. Left again. You went out for a bit. Came back with, eating something. Cooplands bag.

WINNIE. It was a pork and apple roll.

KAYLEIGH *doesn't know what to say.*

KAYLEIGH. Yum.

WINNIE. And you just stood there all that time?

KAYLEIGH. Got dark. Your friend, him –

WINNIE. Stephen.

KAYLEIGH. Stephen comes round with his guitar. I can hear you both singing, see your outlines through the window and that, dancing. Dunno why just, picked this brick up from, this woman's been digging her garden all day, in a right state but. Nearly spring, isn't it? Picked this brick up bloody, lobbed it.

WINNIE *doesn't know what to say.*

STEPHEN *comes back in, with three teas. He hovers in the doorway.*

WINNIE *takes a deep breath.*

WINNIE. Just in time, Stephen, we're all up to date.

KAYLEIGH *looks at* WINNIE.

You have the stripy mug, Kayleigh – thaw you out a bit.

KAYLEIGH. Did you hear all that?

STEPHEN *considers a moment. He nods.*

STEPHEN. I did.

KAYLEIGH. D'you think I'm a twat?

STEPHEN *doesn't say anything.*

You can say, I know I am.

STEPHEN. Not much point me saying then.

KAYLEIGH. I'll pay you back, Winnie, can I call you Winnie? I'll pay you back. For the glass.

WINNIE. That's not the thing.

KAYLEIGH. Thought you'd be mad.

WINNIE. Kayleigh, I'm livid.

KAYLEIGH. Don't seem it.

WINNIE. Well I am.

KAYLEIGH. Oh.

WINNIE. At myself.

KAYLEIGH. Oh.

A moment.

How come?

WINNIE sighs. She holds her hands up like 'doesn't matter'.

She gets up and opens the back door. She takes out her cigarettes, sits on the step and smokes.

KAYLEIGH *mouths to* STEPHEN *'She alright?'*

STEPHEN *doesn't respond.*

KAYLEIGH *doesn't know what to do. She sips her tea.*

Good tea, cheers.

STEPHEN. I'm good at tea.

KAYLEIGH. Good guitaring and all.

STEPHEN. Hardly.

KAYLEIGH. D'you know any Beyoncé?

STEPHEN *shakes his head.*

Good, I literally couldn't give less of a shit about Beyoncé. Am I Bootylicious? No.

A moment.

STEPHEN. What do you like then?

KAYLEIGH. Just, I dunno, like the old songs, like what you were playing and that.

STEPHEN *doesn't believe her.*

STEPHEN. Really.

KAYLEIGH. There's one, this, d'you know this one, hang on, my favourite one it's about like a dirty old town or something? Like 'dirty old town, dirty old town'? Think it's called 'Dirty Old Town'. That's more me. Sometimes I'll just be singing it, looking round like: wow, what a shithole.

STEPHEN *raises his eyebrows.*

D'you know it then?

STEPHEN. Oh.

KAYLEIGH. You must do. You do though. Play us it.

WINNIE. Stephen definitely knows it, Kayleigh.

STEPHEN. Not tonight.

STEPHEN *pulls a face, sort of pushes his guitar away.*

KAYLEIGH. Oh.

WINNIE. Why not tonight?

STEPHEN. Not in the mood.

WINNIE. Well, you're clearly in some sort of mood.

KAYLEIGH. I have said sorry.

WINNIE. Play it, Stephen.

WINNIE *looks at him.*

STEPHEN. I don't want to.

WINNIE. We all do things we don't want to do, Stephen. I spent quite a lot of yesterday hearing about the ins and outs of Mr Whelan's hernia. Honestly, I was this close to knocking him out and operating on it myself. And today's hardly been a walk in the park.

WINNIE *smiles.*

Go on with you. Get playing.

STEPHEN *sighs.*

STEPHEN. I'll strum then. You sing.

He starts to play 'Dirty Old Town' by Ewan MacColl. He nods for KAYLEIGH *to sing.*

She does. Plain and lovely and a bit special. She gets to the second refrain then stops.

KAYLEIGH. Probably stop there.

STEPHEN *stops.*

WINNIE *puts out her cigarette, pulls the back door shut and stands up slowly.*

KAYLEIGH *hugs herself.*

Bit draughty in here.

STEPHEN *looks at the broken window.*

STEPHEN. Wonder why.

KAYLEIGH. Course. Dickhead.

WINNIE. You're not a dickhead, Kayleigh.

In fact by the sounds of it, I owe you an apology.

KAYLEIGH. What you on about?

WINNIE. Behaving like I-don't-know-what in here with you stood outside full of... Must've looked terrible, the dancing, the Guinness. In our defence, we were only cheering ourselves up, it's a hard thing to bury a young man of a Friday, and in my defence, specifically, Stephen chose the song. I actually asked for something holy.

STEPHEN *looks at* WINNIE. *She twinkles.*

But I do think if I'd been in your shoes, Kayleigh, standing outside all day, freezing my arse off, feeling pretty, well, very angry, very very angry at the world and, and at God especially, at the unfairness of, I don't know... If I'd lost my friend in what must seem from where we're all standing really like a horrid, like a waste of a life, I do think, sort of hope really, hope I'd have lobbed a brick through the window as well. At least a brick. If it was Mrs Dale across the road doing her garden I'd say we're lucky not to have got the bird bath.

KAYLEIGH. She moved it this afternoon. Round the back.

WINNIE. Well, I for one will be saying a little prayer of thanks to St Gall, the patron saint of birds, and St Radox, the patron saint of baths.

STEPHEN. Radox? St Radox?

WINNIE. Yes, Stephen. It was a joke.

STEPHEN *raises his eyebrows.*

You're very humourless tonight, Stephen.

He's normally quite fun. You're not getting him at his best.

STEPHEN. I'm just here.

KAYLEIGH. Might be in shock. From the window and that.

STEPHEN *doesn't say anything.*

WINNIE. The point is: I'm sorry, Kayleigh. It must've looked wrong. We must've looked... Disrespectful. When you've lost your friend.

KAYLEIGH. Not my friend I just. Knew him.

WINNIE. Still. We're sorry.

KAYLEIGH *hugs herself again. She's shivering.*

STEPHEN *stands up, very dignified.*

STEPHEN. I might see if there's, used to be a few bits of plywood kicking about out back, we can maybe... mend...

STEPHEN *indicates the window.*

...this.

WINNIE. Good thinking, Batman.

STEPHEN *goes outside.* KAYLEIGH *drains her tea.*

You're free to go, Kayleigh. We don't bear grudges here. Well, you'll have to work on Stephen but I'm all about the forgiveness. Sorry for the shouting, dragging you in.

KAYLEIGH. I will just replace it.

WINNIE. Just like that.

KAYLEIGH. I'll save up.

WINNIE. D'you have a job, Kayleigh?

KAYLEIGH. On and off. Mainly off.

WINNIE. Well, I won't be holding my breath.

KAYLEIGH. I'll sort it.

I broke it, I'll sort it.

WINNIE. Probably done me a favour, to be honest. I've been campaigning for double glazing for, literally, years. Praying for it. St Mark, I say of an evening, double-glaze me. Nothing. But I'm sure the diocese will agree it's hardly worth the hike in insurance when there's a bit of plywood in the shed that'll do the job, for a bit, and then maybe, just maybe... So don't worry about it. It's been lovely to meet you. Re-meet you.

KAYLEIGH *doesn't go.*

Will your mammy not be worried about you?

KAYLEIGH. Doubt it.

WINNIE. Are you sure?

KAYLEIGH. She's dead.

WINNIE. Oh, I'm sorry, Kayleigh, I didn't... Your da then?

KAYLEIGH. Stepdad. Trev.

He'll be right, he's not fussed.

WINNIE. We can stretch to another cup of tea if you're...

WINNIE *goes through to the kitchen.*

Or something to, a sandwich, maybe?

KAYLEIGH. D'you do this a lot? The singing and that.

WINNIE *smiles.*

WINNIE. Friday nights. Guinness, a good sing. Nothing better.

KAYLEIGH. Right.

WINNIE. Our Friday treat.

KAYLEIGH. I bet.

WINNIE. We enjoy it.

KAYLEIGH *nods*.

WINNIE *looks at her*.

I'm wondering something, Kayleigh. I'm wondering: would you like to come join in with us, with the folking? Next week?

KAYLEIGH. Nah.

WINNIE. You seem to like the music.

KAYLEIGH. Yeah but.

WINNIE. You could just come then, join in. No need to chuck any bricks.

KAYLEIGH. I'm probably, I don't know if I'm free.

WINNIE. Well, the offer's there.

STEPHEN *appears in the doorway. He's got a sheet of plywood*.

STEPHEN (*quietly*). Timber.

WINNIE. I was just saying to Kayleigh, she should come next week, join in properly.

STEPHEN. What?

STEPHEN*'s not keen*.

I mean: oh.

Still not keen.

WINNIE. She thinks she might be busy, but…

STEPHEN *is relieved*.

STEPHEN. Oh.

STEPHEN *kicks his Aldi bag. Photocopies of handwritten music and home-made tin whistles fall out.*

Blast.

KAYLEIGH. I can –

STEPHEN. It's alright, if I just…

He leans the plywood against WINNIE, *starts picking his stuff up.* WINNIE *rolls her eyes.*

Mind the, there's glass still.

KAYLEIGH*'s got one of his tin whistles. She is staring at it.*

WINNIE. Stephen made that.

KAYLEIGH. You never.

STEPHEN. Not made made I just…

KAYLEIGH. You actually made it?

STEPHEN. There's, I work at the gas site, Easington there's. Painting, mostly – exterior, maintenance but there's, when they're repairing them, the pipes there's, offcuts or… So I just. It's not hard, it's… Anyway. Um.

STEPHEN *hold his hand out, to try and take it back.* KAYLEIGH *doesn't notice. She's amazed by the tin whistle.*

WINNIE. Perhaps Kayleigh could borrow it, Stephen? Get learning a few tunes.

STEPHEN. Oh.

KAYLEIGH. You're kidding?

WINNIE. Stephen?

WINNIE *smiles at* STEPHEN.

He shrugs.

STEPHEN. If you like.

I mean: have it, if you like.

KAYLEIGH *can't believe it.*

It's in D if that… D-ish.

KAYLEIGH. I'll look after it.

STEPHEN. Worthless, really. Really. Scrap of pipe.

KAYLEIGH *blows the whistle, unimpressively.*

WINNIE *gasps, grins.*

WINNIE. I have just had a Road to Damascus moment.

KAYLEIGH (*confused*). Ace.

WINNIE. Think about it, seriously. Stephen plays guitar, plays whistle. You've got a, a beautiful voice. I've got my spoons. So…

STEPHEN. So?

WINNIE. So: we'll have ourselves a Folk Night. For the Parish. Yes.

STEPHEN. No.

WINNIE. Oh, I can see it now – everyone joining in, full of cake and, drink. A good old-fashioned session.

STEPHEN. The thing is: I don't like, I don't enjoy playing in front of people.

WINNIE. We'll do it at the social centre. Invite everyone – Cubs, WI, Methodists. Easter weekend. We can have a tombola.

STEPHEN. Easter?

WINNIE. We've got a good few weeks, it'll be fine.

KAYLEIGH. I can't even play the whistle yet, Winnie. Like at all.

WINNIE. Stephen'll teach you –

STEPHEN. I won't.

WINNIE. You'll be great. It'll be great.

KAYLEIGH. I'm not sure it will.

WINNIE. It'll be just what we all need after Lent. Think about it: Christ's risen, we've had a Creme Egg, let's belt out 'The Fields of Athenry'. I'll get it in the Parish newsletter tomorrow. Come on now, come on. Get excited.

STEPHEN *is glaring at* WINNIE.

STEPHEN. No.

A moment.

KAYLEIGH. I might go.

WINNIE. Is it far for you? I can drop you back, where is it?

KAYLEIGH. You're alright, I'll just…

WINNIE. The Škoda's outside I can –

KAYLEIGH. You're alright.

KAYLEIGH *goes to the door.*

Cheers for this, Stephen.

She holds up the whistle.

And for not ringing the police.

She gives WINNIE *her phone back.*

WINNIE. See you next week, Kayleigh. I cannot wait.

WINNIE *fist-bumps* KAYLEIGH.

KAYLEIGH. Laters.

KAYLEIGH *leaves.*

STEPHEN *assesses the window and plywood. He doesn't look at* WINNIE.

STEPHEN. Best crack on with this.

WINNIE. Are you cross with me, Stephen?

STEPHEN. Don't be daft.

WINNIE. You don't seem very keen on my amazing plan.

STEPHEN. Not cross.

WINNIE. You sound quite cross.

STEPHEN *sighs.*

STEPHEN. Bit worried about you maybe.

WINNIE. Worried?

STEPHEN. Yes, worried. You've just had a brick pelted at you, glass everywhere, next thing, you're inviting the hooligan who chucked it into your front room.

WINNIE. I know: what am I like?

STEPHEN. An idiot. An absolute –

WINNIE. She's not a hooligan, Stephen, I've known her for years. She was one of the better-behaved ones in junior school.

STEPHEN. Was she?

WINNIE. Made me a Christmas card once – I'll never forget it. A full nativity scene, including two shepherds and an ox, made entirely out of pasta.

STEPHEN. And then... Well.

WINNIE. Out with it.

STEPHEN. You've not said how this afternoon went. Doctor's.

WINNIE. Oh. Right.

Well, the big news is: it's not indigestion. It's angina.

STEPHEN. Crikey.

WINNIE. It's all to do with my heart, my arteries, et cetera.

STEPHEN. Sister.

WINNIE. No wonder the Rennie wasn't helping.

STEPHEN. What now then? Did the doctor say?

WINNIE. She's given me a spray.

WINNIE *shows* STEPHEN.

If I get the pain again, I have to spray it, twice, under my tongue, and then, if it hasn't gone away after five minutes I have to do it again, the spray, and then if it still hasn't gone away, I have to ring an ambulance, cos I'm probably having a heart attack.

STEPHEN. But –

WINNIE. I didn't believe her at first either, Stephen. Told her:
I'm a nun, I'm all heart, there's nothing wrong with my heart.

STEPHEN. What did she say?

WINNIE. She said there is. Said it's a good job you don't drink
or smoke cos if you did you'd be nearing the end of your life
right now.

STEPHEN. But you do drink. You do smoke.

WINNIE. I fibbed.

STEPHEN. You what?

WINNIE. I'm fairly sure she didn't believe me. I had a quick fag
before I went in – calm me down – I think she might've smelt
it. But anyway, they've fitted me in for some tests next week,
in Hull, at the hospital, so we'll know more then. Friday.

STEPHEN. I can try and get it off work, come with you maybe,
if that'd be – ?

WINNIE. No need. I'll just, I'll keep you posted.

STEPHEN *nods*.

And I'll be back, don't worry, for our first practice with
Kayleigh. Won't leave you on your own with a hooligan.

A moment.

STEPHEN. Better get on with this.

He picks up the plywood again.

WINNIE. We're halfway through singing, Stephen. Don't leave
us half-sung.

STEPHEN. Needs doing.

WINNIE. After the singing.

STEPHEN. My dad'll be wondering where I've got to and all.

WINNIE. It's Friday. Your dad knows where you are on a Friday.

STEPHEN*'s not convinced.*

It's all I've been looking forward to all day, Stephen.

STEPHEN *doesn't move.*

Pop your plywood down, let's have a sing.

STEPHEN *smiles.* WINNIE *takes his plywood off him, and props it up to one side.* STEPHEN *gets his guitar out.*

STEPHEN. Go on then.

He plays. WINNIE *sings.*

WINNIE.
And now the storm is over
And we are safe and well
We'll go into a public house –

STEPHEN *and* WINNIE.
And we'll sit and drink like hell!
We will drink strong ale and porter
And make the rafters roar
And when our money is all spent
We'll go to sea once more
FINE GIRL YOU ARE!

2.

Friday night.

The window is patched up with plywood.

STEPHEN *sits alone. He's playing a slow air on a low whistle. It's quiet and delicate, but it's not finished. He goes over a couple of bars, tries different melodies, writes something down.*

KAYLEIGH *comes in.*

KAYLEIGH. Hiya.

> STEPHEN *raises his eyebrows then goes back to his writing.*

> Brought these. For everyone.

> *She puts a packet of already-open hobnobs down on the table.*

> Trev started them but. Quite a few left, so…

> STEPHEN *doesn't look up.*

> Where's Winnie then? I'm feeling folky.

> *A moment.*

> Stephen?

STEPHEN. What's up?

KAYLEIGH. Where's Winnie?

STEPHEN. She's out still. Be here in a bit.

> KAYLEIGH *raises her eyebrows.*

KAYLEIGH. Shit.

STEPHEN. What?

KAYLEIGH. Nowt.

> KAYLEIGH *doesn't know what to do.*

> Might put the kettle on.

STEPHEN. It's just boiled.

KAYLEIGH. Might make a tea then, d'you want a tea?

STEPHEN. No. Actually yes. Please.

KAYLEIGH *goes through to the kitchen. She puts the kettle on again for luck.* STEPHEN *carries on writing down notes. His writing is little and scratchy.*

KAYLEIGH *pops her head back through.*

KAYLEIGH. D'you have milk?

STEPHEN. Um. In the fridge?

KAYLEIGH. No, I know where it is, I just – d'you have milk in your tea?

STEPHEN. Just a bit.

KAYLEIGH. I'll try. I have loads normally. I love milk.

KAYLEIGH *arrives back with two teas.*

It might be too milky.

She passes a mug to STEPHEN.

STEPHEN. It's, great.

It isn't.

Thanks.

KAYLEIGH. Cheers.

KAYLEIGH *tries to clink their mugs together.* STEPHEN *doesn't know what she's doing. It's not a success.*

A moment.

Sounded nice, what you were playing.

STEPHEN *looks down.*

When I came in, you were playing something? On the big one, the low one. Dead slow and that.

STEPHEN *sips his tea.*

What was it?

STEPHEN. Nothing.

KAYLEIGH. Didn't sound like nothing.

STEPHEN. Well.

KAYLEIGH. Will you teach me it? I'm learning as much stuff as I can, that's what I'm doing.

She wiggles her whistle at STEPHEN.

Or just, you know.

Have a go.

STEPHEN. A go?

KAYLEIGH. At teaching me.

STEPHEN. I can't.

KAYLEIGH. Just till Winnie's back. Then she'll sort of, I dunno.

STEPHEN *shakes his head.*

Oh. Right.

KAYLEIGH *sips her tea.*

STEPHEN. Thing is –

KAYLEIGH. No it's fine, honestly. You drink your tea. I'll just stand here, dead quiet and that. Just dead glad I came.

STEPHEN. Can't teach you cos, well, you can't learn it cos. For one thing: it's quite tricky to… Maybe sounds simple cos it's slow and that but, a lot of little, flourishes little, grace notes or what have you so. Takes a while to get the hang of stuff like, like that, you can't just pick it up and… Takes a bit of playing.

KAYLEIGH. Fair enough.

STEPHEN. And also it's not finished yet so –

KAYLEIGH. What you on about? How is it not finished?

STEPHEN. Still working on it.

KAYLEIGH. You're kidding me?

STEPHEN. I don't…

KAYLEIGH. You wrote it?

STEPHEN. It's only half-written.

KAYLEIGH. That is amazing, Stephen.

You just sat down and you just, wrote it?

STEPHEN. Thought, be nice for, something for Sister. Cos it's, well, I don't know what the word is, the real word but it's her sort of anniversary, of taking her vows, becoming a, a nun.

KAYLEIGH. Like a nunniversary?

STEPHEN. Thirty-five years. Next week. Friday.

KAYLEIGH. Shit.

STEPHEN. She's not into sort of fancy things but, this, thought I'd, yeah just, have a go, write her a, a, well. Tune, I suppose. Slow air. 'Winnie's Air'.

KAYLEIGH. That is amazing.

STEPHEN. It isn't.

KAYLEIGH. Honestly, you're my new hero, Stephen. You are.

STEPHEN. What an honour.

KAYLEIGH. I mean it.

STEPHEN. Well, I've enjoyed, I like doing it so…

KAYLEIGH. How d'you do it? I mean like: how?

STEPHEN *shrugs*.

STEPHEN. Just sit and do it.

KAYLEIGH. Like at home or…?

STEPHEN. Maybe. Or maybe at work sometimes. In the breaks. There's a sort of, there's this portakabin for everyone's, for eating your lunch in, sometimes sit outside there with my pack up and, if it's dry, if it's not too cold. Cos you can see right out to sea, there's all, thingies, wind turbines now as well, just. Look at them. Sort of, graceful or. Try stuff out, playing stuff, different stuff. Comes out slow like, like the wind, I suppose. Quite windy round there.

But then, try not to do it at work really, at the moment anyway.

KAYLEIGH. How come?

STEPHEN. Oh, it's…

STEPHEN *shrugs*.

…boring.

KAYLEIGH. I'm interested – how come?

STEPHEN. No it's –

KAYLEIGH. Fuck's sake, Stephen, I'm bloody, trying here, flipping…

STEPHEN *gives* KAYLEIGH *a look, sips his tea*.

Soz.

Not to worry then.

STEPHEN. They've just been taken over again, the company, the whole site. Be looking to get rid of a few, cut down on a few jobs so. Happened a couple of times now, they'll come in, sort of change the signs, wander round with a clipboard, start laying people off. So it's best not to get noticed really. Keep your head down and that. Keep your whistles at home.

KAYLEIGH. Shit.

STEPHEN. Just one of them things.

KAYLEIGH. Yeah but…

STEPHEN. What?

KAYLEIGH. Nowt.

STEPHEN *nods, as if that's an end to the matter. It isn't*.

I mean I came in, before, when I came in, I looked at you and I was like: shit. Cos, you know, face like, well… Not happy. Not pleased to see me.

STEPHEN. That's just my face.

KAYLEIGH. I mean I get it – I wouldn't be pleased, like I did chuck a brick at you but, well, not at you but. But then now I'm just like: going on about everything, making tea and that, you're sitting there just really worried about your future.

STEPHEN. It's fine.

KAYLEIGH. Is it? Thing is, if you lose your job it'll be really hard to get another one round here. Especially at your age.

STEPHEN. Right.

KAYLEIGH. And also Winnie's meant to be here, said she'd be here and she isn't so probably you're allowed to be a bit pissed off with her and all cos you never invited me, did you? Didn't even want me here.

STEPHEN. I never said that.

KAYLEIGH. Not with words.

STEPHEN *looks like he might say something, then stops.*

And then you're writing that tune as well. 'Winnie's Air'.

STEPHEN. What's wrong with that?

KAYLEIGH. Nowt just. It is quite sad. To the point where I'd say it is probably actually depressed.

STEPHEN. Right. Cheers.

KAYLEIGH *offers* STEPHEN *a biscuit.*

KAYLEIGH. Hobnob?

STEPHEN *shakes his head.* KAYLEIGH *takes one.*

STEPHEN. Not long had my tea.

KAYLEIGH. Still eating then. That's something.

STEPHEN. Shall we do some music?

KAYLEIGH. Now?

STEPHEN. Thought you wanted to.

KAYLEIGH. I do but. Hang on, I'll chew, I'll chew.

KAYLEIGH *finishes her biscuit.*

You'll have to teach me.

STEPHEN *shrugs.*

Can't read music but I can either listen to it and figure it out or I can copy your fingers. Or both actually, at the same time's probably best. I've been looking online. The internet is literally full of it.

STEPHEN. Oh.

KAYLEIGH. That's like computers and that.

STEPHEN. I know what the internet is, Kayleigh.

KAYLEIGH. I was winding you.

STEPHEN *sighs*.

Job done.

KAYLEIGH *smiles*.

STEPHEN. Are we doing this then?

KAYLEIGH. We're doing it, we're doing it.

Just do it line by line, and I'll repeat it or something. That's what they do on YouTube. Something cheery though. More cheery.

STEPHEN. Ready?

KAYLEIGH *nods*.

STEPHEN *plays a line of 'Dan O'Keefe's slide'. Very slowly.*

KAYLEIGH *copies it fine.*

STEPHEN *plays the second line. Very slowly.*

KAYLEIGH *copies it. Very easily.*

STEPHEN *plays the last two lines. Quickly. He watches* KAYLEIGH *warily as she repeats them.*

It sounds great.

KAYLEIGH. I love it. What's it called?

STEPHEN. 'Dan O'Keefe's slide'.

KAYLEIGH. Legend.

STEPHEN *is looking at* KAYLEIGH, *trying to figure something out.*

What's up? Have I got hobnob somewhere? I felt a bit fly out.

STEPHEN. You've played that before.

KAYLEIGH. Don't be daft.

STEPHEN. If you already know it, don't need me teaching you.

KAYLEIGH. I don't know anything.

STEPHEN. Sounds like you know it.

KAYLEIGH. Think maybe it's a bit like this one I was doing the other night.

STEPHEN. Let's hear it.

KAYLEIGH. I'll mess it up.

STEPHEN. Well, have a go.

KAYLEIGH. Might do your one first, to practise, like a run-up sort of thing.

KAYLEIGH *plays* STEPHEN*'s tune, faster and more confident, and then properly goes for it with the next tune she's learned.*

It sounds great.

She finishes, and looks a bit uncertain.

STEPHEN *doesn't say anything. He is looking at* KAYLEIGH *again, trying to figure her out.*

KAYLEIGH *sighs.*

That good, eh? Fair enough.

STEPHEN. 'Brian Boru's March' was that?

KAYLEIGH *shrugs.*

KAYLEIGH. Dunno what it's called. Just like it.

STEPHEN. There's different sort of, depending who you hear it from. You make it your own, hear it and, and, that's just, that's folk but...

STEPHEN *plays a couple of bars on the whistle.*

He nods.

That's the one, I reckon.

WINNIE *enters.*

She looks drained.

WINNIE. Don't ask.

STEPHEN. Sister, is everything – ?

WINNIE. Hobnobs. There's a sight for sore eyes.

WINNIE *sits down and closes her eyes.*

Been looking forward to this all day. Heavenly shout out to St Nicholas of Myra, the patron saint of chairs.

STEPHEN. Are you alright?

WINNIE *opens her eyes.*

WINNIE. I'm livid.

STEPHEN. Bad day?

WINNIE. Oh, it was fine. I mean: not fine fine – everything's… (*To* KAYLEIGH.) I've been at the hospital, Kayleigh. I don't know if Stephen said.

KAYLEIGH. Oh.

KAYLEIGH *shakes her head.*

WINNIE. Getting some tests done.

KAYLEIGH. What's the matter?

WINNIE. Mostly, angina. Which for some reason I keep calling: vagina. It doesn't help.

KAYLEIGH. I don't know what that means. The first one.

WINNIE. It means, Kayleigh, no more fun. No more drinking, no more getting worked up, no more smoking, apparently – I'm ignoring that, obviously but.

STEPHEN. Sister.

WINNIE. I'm getting pills, blood-thinners. They've showered me with leaflets.

WINNIE *gets some leaflets out of her bag.*

And I've got my spray, of course.

WINNIE *squirts the spray like perfume.*

STEPHEN. This does all sound quite serious.

WINNIE. The consultant basically said I could pop my clogs at any moment. Added to which: he was a very pale man, heavy-breather – I did wonder briefly if he might actually be Death, come to get me. But then one of the other doctors popped in, called him Nigel, mentioned something about badminton so I thought: probably not. It's hard to imagine the Grim Reaper with a shuttlecock.

KAYLEIGH. D'you want a cup of tea?

WINNIE. Oh, I'd love one. Thank you, Kayleigh.

KAYLEIGH *goes through to the kitchen.*

STEPHEN. So. Not a brilliant day.

WINNIE. That's not the worst bit, Stephen.

STEPHEN. Oh.

WINNIE. Picture this: I've been through all the sitting, the waiting, spent three pounds thirty-nine on a mediocre sandwich, been wired up to a monitor, jogged, et cetera, I've been jiggled about, prodded, pressed with some very chilly instruments, got released, finally, back into the world, with my clogged-up arteries and uncertain future, I'm in the lift going down, who should I bump in to? Who should get into the lift with me on floor number seven? I'll give you a clue: he's got a fucking hernia.

STEPHEN. Oh dear.

WINNIE. And did he ask how I was?

STEPHEN. No?

WINNIE. No. He spotted me, took a deep breath, launched into another two-hour rant about what a rough deal it is – whinging, complaining, whining. I mean, I know it's not nice to have a bit of your stomach lining poking out, I get it, I do, but really – how much more is there to say?

STEPHEN. You could put him in the bidding prayers. Might shut him up.

WINNIE. Geraldine's put me in the bidding prayers back home.
I told her: don't be making a fuss now. She says if your own
sister can't make a fuss of you when you've got a dodgy
heart, who can? Wants me to go stay with them for a bit.

STEPHEN. D'you think you will?

WINNIE *shakes her head.*

WINNIE. Anyway, I'm sorry to be so late back. And I'm sorry
to have missed you both playing.

KAYLEIGH *gives* WINNIE *her tea.*

KAYLEIGH. You haven't missed much.

WINNIE. These things take time, poppet. I'm sure it'll sound
lovely by the time our Easter Folk Night comes round.

STEPHEN. If.

WINNIE. I'm afraid it's a when, Stephen. I've told Mr Whelan
about it.

STEPHEN. What?

WINNIE. Says he'll sort the posters for us. Apparently, he's got
a laminator.

STEPHEN. No.

WINNIE. Oh, for –

STEPHEN. I said: no. I said no when you were talking about it
before, I'm saying it again. No.

WINNIE. Stephen.

STEPHEN. What?

WINNIE. You're being stubborn.

STEPHEN. Says you.

WINNIE. Exactly. We can't both be stubborn, can we? Not
when we disagree. You love the folk.

STEPHEN. I love the music, playing the music, with you, just
us, I don't love, strangers, new people, listening. Don't know
why, suddenly, you're getting, loads of people –

WINNIE. It won't be loads of people, it'll be maybe twenty, thirty –

STEPHEN. Thirty.

WINNIE. I knew you'd be like this.

STEPHEN. Cos you shouldn't be doing it.

WINNIE. Nearly spring, Stephen. Fresh start. Let's try new things.

STEPHEN. I'm not keen.

WINNIE. D'you know what I've been thinking about a lot just lately, Stephen? The parable of the talents. No, don't roll your eyes. Cos you can bury your talents, like the fella in the parable, who, he's the baddie really, of the parable, is the thing. Or, you can share your talents, grow them a bit, have everyone enjoying them, like the goodie. That's what you should do. What we all should do.

I've thought of a brilliant tagline, for the posters, Mr Whelan approved: 'What. The. Folk?' I've seen it before, on leaflets et cetera.

Come on, Stephen. Come on, come on, come on.

STEPHEN *glares at* WINNIE.

KAYLEIGH *doesn't know what to do*.

KAYLEIGH. We should sing something.

STEPHEN *is still glaring at* WINNIE.

I liked it last week. The singing.

WINNIE *smiles at* KAYLEIGH.

WINNIE. That's a lovely idea, Kayleigh.

Something hopeful. Get the nights drawing out and the world back on its feet, just a bit. How about...?

WINNIE *sings the first line of 'The Wild Mountain Thyme' by Francis McPeake*.

Join in, Stephen. Stephen.

STEPHEN *plays a chord.*

And you, Kayleigh. Do you know it? Join in.

KAYLEIGH *joins in and sings the first verse with* WINNIE.

Come on now, Stephen. Chorus.

WINNIE *and* KAYLEIGH *sing the chorus.* STEPHEN
doesn't join in.

You're not joining in very much.

STEPHEN *gives in and sings the second verse by himself.*
KAYLEIGH *takes the third verse, with* WINNIE *and*
STEPHEN *joining in on the chorus.*

Big finish now.

They all sing the chorus again.

There now, isn't that better?

STEPHEN *doesn't seem any cheerier.*

STEPHEN. Think I'm done. For tonight.

STEPHEN *starts to put his guitar away.*

WINNIE. Stephen.

STEPHEN. Better check on my dad.

WINNIE. Stephen, come on now.

STEPHEN. Left him in charge of a cottage pie. Microwave.
Anything could happen.

WINNIE. I'll send a little memo to St Jude.

STEPHEN *doesn't smile.*

(*To* KAYLEIGH.) Lost causes.

STEPHEN. Might take some of these, if that's alright?

STEPHEN *picks up some of* WINNIE's *leaflets.*

WINNIE. If you like. It's all doom and gloom, from what I can
make out.

STEPHEN. Right.

KAYLEIGH. I'm heading back that way and all, we can walk together.

STEPHEN. Oh.

STEPHEN *isn't keen*.

WINNIE. Lovely. Great. Sleep tight then, Stephen.

STEPHEN *leaves*.

Kayleigh.

KAYLEIGH. Don't worry, Winnie – I've got this.

KAYLEIGH *leaves*.

WINNIE *sits down. Her chest hurts. She takes her spray.*

3.

Friday night.

STEPHEN *and* KAYLEIGH *are waiting for* WINNIE *to arrive.*

STEPHEN*'s brought some food, in a tin.* KAYLEIGH*'s made a banner and stuck it up on the wall. It says 'HAPPY NUNNIVERSARY'* .

WINNIE *comes in.*

WINNIE. Heavens above.

STEPHEN *and* KAYLEIGH (*quietly*). Surprise.

WINNIE. What's this?

STEPHEN. It's um, your, your nunniversary.

WINNIE. Oh, it's lovely, it is lovely. Thank you.

KAYLEIGH. Stephen said just keep it quite a quiet surprise, cos you're not meant to have big shocks.

WINNIE. What d'you mean?

KAYLEIGH *shrugs.*

KAYLEIGH. And then, we've both got you presents.

WINNIE. Crikey.

KAYLEIGH. Just songs, nothing exciting.

WINNIE. Oh, I love a good song.

KAYLEIGH. I'll go first. Stephen's doing the chords.

STEPHEN *gets his guitar ready.* KAYLEIGH *looks nervous.*

I'm just off to the loo first actually. Just a sec.

WINNIE *grins at* STEPHEN.

STEPHEN. What's up?

WINNIE. D'you know, Stephen, I've been a nun for thirty-five years now – you're the only person who remembers this. Ever. Thank you.

STEPHEN *looks pleased.*

STEPHEN. Kayleigh's idea. The banner and that.

WINNIE. Really?

STEPHEN. Reckons we should have a sort of, singalong and, and nibbles, if it goes well it can be like a practice run. For your Easter Folk Night.

WINNIE. Our Easter Folk Night, Stephen.

And this, what's this?

STEPHEN. Just something small.

WINNIE. Looks like a cake to me.

STEPHEN. It isn't.

A toilet flushes.

WINNIE. Here we go.

KAYLEIGH *comes downstairs.*

KAYLEIGH. You ready then?

WINNIE *sits down comfy.*

WINNIE. I can't wait.

KAYLEIGH. Right.

She is a bit flustered.

WINNIE. Everything alright, Kayleigh?

KAYLEIGH. Oh yeah, I just. I have to do this now or I never will.

WINNIE nods.

WINNIE. Okay.

KAYLEIGH. You start, Stephen, I'll join in.

STEPHEN nods.

Also, um, Winnie, can you just look after that? Just for a minute please.

KAYLEIGH passes something to WINNIE. It's a pregnancy test.

Actually, three minutes. Right: song. Go.

STEPHEN doesn't know what to do.

STEPHEN. Um.

KAYLEIGH. Like strum... Strum....

He starts to play, quietly.

KAYLEIGH sings the first verse and chorus of 'Bring Me a Boat' by Kate Rusby.

WINNIE. Kayleigh.

KAYLEIGH. Just hang on to it, Winnie, if you will.

WINNIE. But –

KAYLEIGH holds up a finger. She sings the second verse.

WINNIE is trying to give KAYLEIGH the pregnancy test.

KAYLEIGH. Nearly there, Winnie. Last chorus.

WINNIE keeps hold of it.

KAYLEIGH sings the chorus.

STEPHEN stops.

WINNIE. Kayleigh.

WINNIE gives KAYLEIGH the test.

KAYLEIGH. Thought so.

Thought it was a nice song anyway. Bit sad and that but...
Happy Nunniversary, anyway.

KAYLEIGH looks at the test.

It's fine. Four months off my period. Five to go. Bonus.

WINNIE. Four months?

KAYLEIGH. Bit slow on the uptake. Thought I'd just skipped
one, how you do, and then I just thought my ovaries must be
resting. And then I think I probably knew deep down but I
wasn't ready to know sort of thing.

She wiggles the test.

Shoplifted this. Lloyds pharmacy.

Who is Lloyd?

STEPHEN *shrugs.*

WINNIE. Are you alright, Kayleigh?

KAYLEIGH gives WINNIE a thumbs-up.

KAYLEIGH. We should do party stuff really. Stephen – still got
to play yours.

STEPHEN. Now doesn't feel like the time.

KAYLEIGH. Suppose not.

WINNIE. Well, I need a smoke.

WINNIE gets her cigarettes out.

I'll breathe outside, I promise.

She lights up.

And you're sure? You're absolutely –

KAYLEIGH nods.

KAYLEIGH. Explains a lot actually.

WINNIE. If you don't want to talk about it…

KAYLEIGH. That alright?

WINNIE. Of course, of course.

WINNIE *smokes*.

KAYLEIGH *plays with the test, anxiously*.

KAYLEIGH. Okay, we'll talk about it.

WINNIE. A question.

KAYLEIGH. Yep.

WINNIE. Well, I think you should go to the doctor's.

KAYLEIGH. That's not a question.

WINNIE. But you will though?

KAYLEIGH *nods*.

KAYLEIGH. Monday. I'll ring up Monday.

WINNIE. Do you know whose baby it is?

KAYLEIGH. Course I do, Winnie. It's God's.

A moment.

WINNIE. I'm sorry, I'm being nosy, none of my business.

KAYLEIGH. It's Jason. I mean it was Jason. Before, yeah. Before he crashed his car and, you know, died and that. We were sort of… I mean, we weren't, not really just. Couple of, well, few times but. But it was a bit weird cos I'm only fifteen and that. And also I think he had a girlfriend probably. I mean, there was, she went to his funeral I think so. Looked well upset.

Felt quite bad for her really. To be honest.

WINNIE *puts her cigarette out*.

WINNIE. Oh, Kayleigh.

KAYLEIGH. Yeah. Fucking… Might just…

KAYLEIGH *goes upstairs and locks herself in the bathroom*.

WINNIE *looks at* STEPHEN.

She follows KAYLEIGH *upstairs, and knocks on the door.*

WINNIE. Things alright in there? I mean, not alright alright, obviously, big day, big news day but just, right enough?

Silence.

I'll just be this side of the door then, if you need me. On the stairs.

WINNIE *sits on the top step.*

Maybe Stephen might play his song, that he's done? Hint.

STEPHEN. Not really the right thing for, for now.

Not so cheery, maybe. And also, not ready, quite, maybe.

WINNIE. For crying out loud, Stephen, play the bastard.

STEPHEN. I have, we could, I could open the, if you like?

STEPHEN *picks up his biscuit tin.*

WINNIE. I'm not sure now's quite the time for a cake, Stephen.

STEPHEN. No it's, um, I was reading through your leaflets, the leaflets they gave you, about your heart and so on, it said a good thing was, well, a good thing to do was sort of, a good thing to think about was sort of: mediterranean diet. Which is, lots of fruit, vegetables, olive oil instead of... Bit of dairy, bits and bobs, and then: eggs, fish. So: one of the things it suggested, one of the recipes in the leaflet. Well. I've made you a frittata. In case you sort of. Well. Just in case.

WINNIE. Stephen, if now isn't the moment for a cake, I'm absolutely certain it's not the time for a frittata. Will you please just play. The bloody. Song.

KAYLEIGH *opens the door, and comes out.*

KAYLEIGH. Don't play it now.

She sits down on a step as well.

WINNIE. Oh.

KAYLEIGH. It's special. Winnie, you've got to listen properly. Stephen's like actually, well, it's, should be special and I've just, I've basically, I've ruined it.

WINNIE. Nonsense.

KAYLEIGH. No I actually have.

STEPHEN *holds out the tin*.

STEPHEN. Frittata?

KAYLEIGH. Um. I don't know what that is.

STEPHEN. It's like a sort of quiche, without the pastry. Eggy.

KAYLEIGH. Oh.

KAYLEIGH *shakes her head*.

Not sure if, think maybe I shouldn't have eggs.

STEPHEN *puts the tin down*.

WINNIE. Let's start with the good news, Kayleigh.

The good news is you've got a choice in terms of patron saint for mothers, you've got St Monica, or if she's busy, pop along the corridor, St Anne. Both lovely saints, in case you fancy the odd bit of praying. And Mary's probably up for it as well, unofficial-like.

KAYLEIGH. Good to know. Cheers.

WINNIE. And I'm here too, if you need...

WINNIE *looks at* KAYLEIGH.

Is there someone at school you could, a teacher or – ?

KAYLEIGH. Oh, I don't go to school.

WINNIE. Everyone goes to school.

KAYLEIGH. It's nothing bad, I just, thought I'd just stop going for a bit. In like September.

Sort of a test, see how long it took them to notice. But then they just haven't noticed.

But I'm not fussed, I hated it anyway. It was mostly just being bad at stuff.

WINNIE *makes a decision.*

WINNIE. Right.

KAYLEIGH. What?

WINNIE *gets a key that's hanging up.*

WINNIE. I'd like to give you this, Kayleigh.

WINNIE *holds the key out to* KAYLEIGH.

STEPHEN. Sister, hang on.

WINNIE. What?

STEPHEN. Are you sure that's a good plan?

WINNIE. I'm sure.

And you should know, Kayleigh, you're welcome here, any time. Alright? Always room at this inn.

KAYLEIGH *doesn't take the key.*

It's the front door. You have to jiggle it a bit.

KAYLEIGH. You don't have to give me a key to your house.

STEPHEN. You really don't.

WINNIE. I know. But I'll feel better knowing you've got somewhere to come. Just in case. Sometimes these things, explaining these things to, well, to your family or –

KAYLEIGH. Not telling Trev.

WINNIE. D'you think that's wise?

KAYLEIGH. Don't give a shit if it's wise, I'm not telling him.

WINNIE. D'you not think he might notice anyway?

KAYLEIGH. I actually doubt it.

WINNIE. Well. There's a camp bed upstairs if you need it. In case I'm not about or...

STEPHEN *is gathering up his belongings. He notices*
WINNIE *has stopped talking. She is looking at him.*

Where are you going, all of a sudden?

STEPHEN. Home. Need to check on my dad. And also I think
you're an idiot.

WINNIE. Why?

STEPHEN. Can't just go handing out your house keys, willy-
nilly, Sister. Barely know her.

WINNIE. Stephen –

STEPHEN. Not safe, for a start.

KAYLEIGH. You don't have to, honestly. I don't need –

WINNIE. Kayleigh, it's fine.

STEPHEN. Oh, it's fine, is it? Good. Fine. You just give
someone you hardly know, who chucks bricks at you –

KAYLEIGH. Not at you.

STEPHEN. Just give her a key to your house, and that's fine.

WINNIE. I gave one to you.

STEPHEN. So I could water your geraniums. Keep an eye on
things, when you were back home. Years ago.

STEPHEN*'s gathered his stuff up.*

WINNIE. Come on now, Stephen. Don't go. Stay. Have some
frittata.

STEPHEN. No I don't think I will.

WINNIE. Well, at least play me your tune.

STEPHEN *shakes his head.*

STEPHEN (*to* KAYLEIGH). She doesn't need trouble from
you. Alright?

KAYLEIGH *looks wide-eyed.*

KAYLEIGH. Alright.

STEPHEN *nods*.

STEPHEN. I'm leaving now cos... Cos I am.

WINNIE. Stephen.

STEPHEN *leaves*.

KAYLEIGH. D'you think you should go after him?

WINNIE. Let him go.

KAYLEIGH. This does sort of feel like my fault.

WINNIE. No, Kayleigh.

KAYLEIGH. And yours, a bit.

WINNIE. My fault?

KAYLEIGH. We all know you're iller than you're letting on, you just are.

WINNIE. Oh.

KAYLEIGH. Now you're like forcing the Easter Folk Night on him.

WINNIE. It'll be fun. Do him good. All of us.

KAYLEIGH. D'you think?

WINNIE. I do.

Wanted to tell him I've thought of a name for the band as well.

KAYLEIGH. Have you?

WINNIE. The Shenanigans. Think about it: a night of shenanigans with The Shenanigans.

KAYLEIGH. What sort of shenanigans?

WINNIE. Well, as I've said, a tombola, et cetera.

KAYLEIGH *smiles*.

KAYLEIGH. Sounds good.

WINNIE. Faint praise.

KAYLEIGH. I think you should go check if he's alright.

WINNIE. More worried about you to be honest, Kayleigh.

KAYLEIGH. What you on about?

WINNIE. Well…

WINNIE *gestures towards* KAYLEIGH*'s pregnancy.*

KAYLEIGH. Oh.

WINNIE. Though I'm not massively experienced in this department, I have to say. Not had many babies. Never even got as far as a kiss before all this nun stuff happened so.

KAYLEIGH. You're kidding?

WINNIE. No.

KAYLEIGH. You've literally never kissed anyone? Never?

WINNIE. Not kissed kissed.

KAYLEIGH. Shit.

WINNIE. What?

KAYLEIGH. Nowt, just… Nuns.

WINNIE. Little secret, Kayleigh – I was a bit of a wallflower, pre-nun. Quiet little thing really, with my rosary beads. Then this happened and bam. I just sort of got the hang of things, a bit. Right in the middle, getting stuck in, out of my depth completely but having a go at least. Not sure Stephen's ever got the hang of things, not really. You'd think he'd love to be playing his music, have all those people enjoying his music but.

WINNIE *shakes her head.*

Scared to be noticed, I think. Not quite ready to be seen.

KAYLEIGH. Shut your eyes.

WINNIE. What?

KAYLEIGH. Just please just, close them. Close your eyes.

WINNIE *does.*

A moment.

KAYLEIGH *kisses her, gently, on the lips.*

WINNIE *pulls away.*

WINNIE. Oh, Kayleigh.

KAYLEIGH. Just want you to know what it feels like.

WINNIE. No, Kayleigh.

KAYLEIGH. I'm sixteen, you're not a paedo. Well, fifteen.

WINNIE. That isn't –

KAYLEIGH. I just think all that sort of, all that life, being busy and, and doing stuff, all that but, this is the thing. How it feels when someone's just, there, in front of you and just, I dunno, with you, completely with you. This is the thing.

WINNIE. And that, Kayleigh, that is why you must never, ever become a nun.

Promise me.

WINNIE *stands up, pats* KAYLEIGH *on the top of her head.*

God bless.

KAYLEIGH *is embarrassed.*

KAYLEIGH. I might, um. Go.

WINNIE. You're alright? You'll be alright.

KAYLEIGH. Yeah, course.

KAYLEIGH *goes to leave.*

WINNIE *picks up the key.*

WINNIE. Just in case.

She holds it out.

KAYLEIGH *smiles, takes it.*

4.

Tuesday afternoon.

STEPHEN*'s holding a poster for the Easter Folk Night in front of* WINNIE.

It is laminated.

STEPHEN. Explain.

WINNIE. It's all on the poster, Stephen. Time, date, venue. Our new name. Mr Whelan said he'd sort them and I have to say I wasn't expecting much, but he's outdone himself this time, he really has. So glossy.

STEPHEN. It's got a phone number on.

WINNIE. Just for any sort of, ticket enquiries.

STEPHEN. My phone number.

WINNIE. You must've taken this one down from somewhere, have you?

STEPHEN. Shores Centre.

WINNIE. Maybe you'll pop it back up for me? No rush. Just next time you're passing.

STEPHEN. Should've checked, should've asked me before you put my phone number on.

WINNIE. I thought you'd say no.

STEPHEN. Exactly.

WINNIE. No point asking then, was there.

STEPHEN. I want you to take them down.

WINNIE. Don't be silly now, Stephen.

STEPHEN. All of them. And take my number off them.

WINNIE. Why?

STEPHEN. I've said a hundred times, I'm not doing your Easter Bloody Folk Night.

WINNIE. Language, Stephen.

STEPHEN. I'm not playing guitar, I'm not playing whistle, I'm not answering the phone, selling tickets. I'm not.

WINNIE. There's no need to get angry.

STEPHEN. You always do this.

WINNIE. Organise a folk night? I do not. This is literally the first time.

STEPHEN. Have a go at me for getting angry, have a go at me for getting angry when you're very clearly in the wrong.

WINNIE. Look, Stephen, no one's pretending I'm not in the wrong. That's a given. I'm meddlesome and interfering and I take liberties and, all that. But I'm also your friend. And I really do think getting out there, playing your music, with some nice people from church, I really do think it'll do you the world of good. All of us. And I just thought, I'm not here for a couple of weeks, thought you wouldn't mind answering the phone a few times while I'm away. I thought it sounded, not asking much. Very doable.

STEPHEN. What d'you mean, you're not here?

WINNIE. Going over to Ireland. Last-minute trip.

STEPHEN. When?

WINNIE. In about ten minutes. Mr Whelan's picking me up, dropping me off at the station. Can't wait for the hernia updates.

STEPHEN. You never said.

WINNIE. Well, it's all happened very suddenly, Stephen. Geraldine's booked me a train Hull to Manchester and then a flight. And then I bumped into Mr Whelan in Tesco, he's insisting on giving me a lift to the station, even though I've repeatedly asked him not to. It's one of those times you just have to go with it. That's being a nun.

STEPHEN. Is everything alright? With your sister, I mean.

WINNIE. I got a pain while she was on the phone, couple of nights ago, had to use my spray. And then her friend from over-fifties pilates, she's a nurse somewhere, between her and Doctor Google they've decided I'm absolutely on my last legs, won't believe I'm alright, won't believe I'm looking after myself, et cetera. I mentioned a cheese and onion pasty, she hit the roof.

STEPHEN. You're not looking after yourself. Not really.

WINNIE. They're on at me to quit the ciggies as well. Fat chance.

I told her I've read the leaflets, Geraldine. It basically says: if your number's up, it's up.

STEPHEN. That isn't quite what the leaflets say.

WINNIE. Long story short, they're forcing a bit of TLC on me. Which I suppose might be alright. Just for a week or so. And you're in charge of our Easter Folk Night. Just till I'm back. It'll all be fine.

STEPHEN. It'll all be fine for you, you won't be here.

WINNIE. No, Stephen, I'll be on the outskirts of Cork, covered in nicotine patches.

STEPHEN. I just think it's quite a lot to, to put on me, another headache, on top of –

WINNIE. On top of what, exactly? Painting some pipes. Come now, Stephen.

STEPHEN. I won't be painting pipes, actually. I'll be looking for a new job.

WINNIE. Oh. Shit.

STEPHEN. Finally found a machine that can do a better job than us so, they're investing in that instead. More efficient.

WINNIE. Stephen, I didn't know.

STEPHEN. So I'll just be stuck at home really, with my dad to look after. He can criticise my cooking and so on, tell me yet again what a success Alan's made of his life in Bristol, how well he's doing. Watch the odd episode of *Pointless*. That sort of thing.

WINNIE. All the more reason to focus on the folk.

STEPHEN. I've run out of things to say.

WINNIE*'s chest is hurting.*

She sits down.

WINNIE. Shit.

STEPHEN. What's the matter?

WINNIE. Stephen, would you pass...?

WINNIE *indicates her spray.*

STEPHEN. Here, here.

WINNIE. Just...

WINNIE *is sitting down now. She sprays underneath her tongue.*

Thank you.

Takes a minute. To work. Hopefully.

STEPHEN. Is there anything I can, I can do?

WINNIE *shakes her head.*

Any water or anything?

WINNIE *shakes her head.*

She closes her eyes.

A few seconds pass.

The pain eases, gradually.

WINNIE. You could help with the Easter Folk Night.

STEPHEN. No.

KAYLEIGH *knocks.*

WINNIE. It's open.

KAYLEIGH *comes in.*

KAYLEIGH. Hiya.

I just, I brought this to –

KAYLEIGH*'s got a photo of her scan to show them.*

WINNIE. Don't mind us, Kayleigh, we're just falling out.

KAYLEIGH. What?

WINNIE. Stephen's normally quite good at keeping his mouth shut. Not today.

KAYLEIGH *puts the photo back in her pocket.*

WINNIE *and* STEPHEN *are both quiet.*

KAYLEIGH. Seen a couple of posters up. For the Easter Folk Night. Look immense.

WINNIE. See?

STEPHEN *gets up to go.*

STEPHEN. I'm not doing this now. I'll just let the phone ring, Sister. You can sort it when you're back.

WINNIE. Fine.

KAYLEIGH. Where are you going?

WINNIE. Ireland. In about five minutes.

A few more of my nearest and dearest are hoping they can have a go at my lifestyle choices, just for kicks. No, it's great actually, I'm not feeling like I'm getting attacked enough for smoking, eating pastry, enjoying my life, et cetera. When all I really need is a bit of help.

It's not often, is it, I ask for a bit of help?

STEPHEN. You didn't ask.

WINNIE. Don't be cross, Stephen.

STEPHEN. I am cross though. I am.

I don't need people ringing up about, I don't even know why we're doing the Easter Folk Night, it's a terrible idea, nobody wants it in the first place, you've not sold any tickets. And then, you're just off to Ireland, just suddenly off to Ireland, not telling us you're going just, going. Which if anything has made me more worried about you, if I'm honest. And I'm already, you know, quite worried, so. So I'm mad really.

WINNIE. Stephen.

WINNIE *tries to touch* STEPHEN*'s arm.*

STEPHEN. No. Just let me be mad.

WINNIE *doesn't know what to do.*

KAYLEIGH. You shouldn't be cross if you're not seeing each other for a bit.

That's what I think anyway.

WINNIE. Exactly.

KAYLEIGH. Especially cos, you know.

Cos you just never know, do you? Is the thing.

Like I remember with my mum, once I knew she was ill like not-getting-better ill I just got sort of obsessed with never falling out with her. To the point where it was weird and a bit strained and she had to have this chat with me, sort of reassuring me that if we'd had cross words or something and then I didn't see her again before she died she still definitely knew that I loved her. Dunno why, she just said it. But then we never fell out any more after that so. Job done.

And like, a lot of the time now when I'm thinking about Jason and that, cos I'm thinking about him quite a lot at the moment, we did not have that thing where we sort of parted nicely, like I think he just called me a slag or something and then I cried and told him his dick was a weird shape, which it wasn't actually, it was a lovely shape, but that is literally how we left it. And I regret that really, cos now he's dead and that, but I've got like his little son or daughter growing inside me. So probably it is best to just be nice to each other. Just like sort of in case.

A moment.

STEPHEN. Shall we have a sing, while you wait for Mr Whelan?

WINNIE *smiles.*

WINNIE. Go on then.

Our usual?

STEPHEN *smiles*.

He starts to play the chords, for 'If I Should Fall from Grace with God' by Shane MacGowan.

STEPHEN. Is it worth? There's sort of a whistle bit you, if you can sort of pick it up? I don't know.

KAYLEIGH. Yes!

She is looking for her whistle, through her bag.

STEPHEN. It's sort of…

STEPHEN *hums the whistle bit*. KAYLEIGH *picks it up*.

WINNIE. I'll crack these out. With a bit of help from St Peter Damian. Genuinely, genuinely, the patron saint of spoons.

She's got some spoons.

As WINNIE sings, KAYLEIGH picks out moments to join in with bits of tin whistle. WINNIE sings the first verse and chorus.

Kayleigh, that whistle is lovely. Lovely.

KAYLEIGH. Keep going.

WINNIE sings the second verse and chorus.

WINNIE. Come on, you two, last bit all together.

They all sing the last verse and chorus together.

A car horn beeps outside. WINNIE looks through the window.

That's my lift. Not coming to the door, I suspect.

KAYLEIGH. Charming.

WINNIE picks up her bag.

STEPHEN. I'll take that.

WINNIE. Don't be daft, I'm fine.

You'll lock up for me?

STEPHEN. Oh, oh, course.

The horn beeps again.

WINNIE *checks around the room.*

WINNIE. Right.

Look after each other. Okay? While I'm away. Look after each other.

She opens the door, and leaves.

5.

Night.

A fortnight has passed.

STEPHEN *unlocks the door, comes in.*

He's got his old carrier bag full of music and tin whistles, and he's got some cans of Guinness.

He goes into the kitchen to get two glasses.

He opens two cans of Guinness and pours them out.

He sits down and searches through his bag for a tatty piece of manuscript paper and his low whistle.

Meanwhile, KAYLEIGH *is creeping downstairs with a statue of St Francis held like a baseball bat.*

She spots STEPHEN.

KAYLEIGH. Fucking hell, Stephen.

STEPHEN *jumps.*

Scared the shit out of me.

STEPHEN. Well. You, you too.

KAYLEIGH. Soz, sorry.

A moment.

Pop you down, St Francis of Assisi.

KAYLEIGH *puts the statue down.*

She looks at STEPHEN.

You alright?

STEPHEN *nods.*

STEPHEN. Just thought…

KAYLEIGH. Last drink. Goodbye.

I've ruined that.

STEPHEN. It's –

KAYLEIGH. No, I have, what a dick, sorry.

STEPHEN. What are you doing here?

KAYLEIGH. Oh, nothing, nowt just. You know. Just reading actually. Loads of books upstairs. There's like a dictionary of saints.

STEPHEN. I meant.

KAYLEIGH. Oh, I live here now so…

STEPHEN. You live here?

KAYLEIGH. Just for a bit, yeah. Just while stuff sort of calms down.

STEPHEN. What stuff? What's happened?

KAYLEIGH. Nowt it's fine.

STEPHEN. Really?

KAYLEIGH. Really.

Cos, I had a key and that and, figured, no one else is using it. No one'll mind. I'd've warned you if I'd known sort of thing.

STEPHEN. Thought you were with your, stepdad or…

KAYLEIGH. Trev says if I'm old enough to be getting pregnant I'm old enough to sort myself out, somewhere to live and that. Which, turns out, true cos. Here I am.

He figured it out. Well, I mean, I told him.

Went down really well. Obvs.

STEPHEN. Can't live here, Kayleigh.

KAYLEIGH. Well, I am doing.

STEPHEN. The church folks'll be here soon, to sort everything. Tomorrow, maybe. They'll all be here for, well, for the service.

KAYLEIGH. Bet they will. Never miss a good funeral, do they? I mean it's not even a funeral, is it? The ashes, scatter the ashes.

I like that. Like to think of her just sort of whizzing about. Getting breathed and that.

STEPHEN. Won't let you just stay.

KAYLEIGH. I'll be right.

STEPHEN. They really won't let you.

KAYLEIGH. Be fine.

STEPHEN. They're not all Sister Winnie, you know.

KAYLEIGH *shrugs*.

KAYLEIGH. Not doing any harm.

STEPHEN. I know.

KAYLEIGH. And I'm not off back to Trev's, he's a fucking…

STEPHEN. Oh.

KAYLEIGH. I mean if he apologised or whatever, yes, maybe but. For now, might as well just stay here till they kick me out to be honest. Have a think. New plan.

STEPHEN. Right. Right.

KAYLEIGH. What about you though?

STEPHEN. What d'you mean?

KAYLEIGH. You alright?

STEPHEN *shrugs*.

It's just this, last drink, last Guinness, in the dark and that…

STEPHEN. What?

KAYLEIGH. Well. Nowt.

I mean, it is quite a sad thing to do. Stephen.

Like I feel like you're probably quite sad.

STEPHEN. I just… Tomorrow'll be, everyone. Thought this'd be, this is just us.

KAYLEIGH. Apart from I'm here.

STEPHEN. Well.

A moment.

I'm really glad you got us to sing that song together, Kayleigh. That was, a lovely thing.

KAYLEIGH *shrugs*.

KAYLEIGH. Just what we do, isn't it?

I'm guessing the Easter Folk Night's off.

STEPHEN *smiles*.

STEPHEN. Well, thought maybe we could, maybe do one in the summer. When we've had a bit of time and that. Learned some stuff. Ready.

KAYLEIGH. Teach me something now.

STEPHEN *shakes his head*.

He sips his Guinness.

He sighs.

Did you love her?

STEPHEN. What?

KAYLEIGH. I always thought, probably, you loved her.

It's alright if you did. I'm not judging. I think love is, yeah. Brilliant, actually.

Don't I?

KAYLEIGH *strokes her tummy*.

Only thing I'm any good at. Turns out.

STEPHEN. You're good at, at your whistle.

KAYLEIGH. Well.

STEPHEN. Better than me.

KAYLEIGH. Thing is, Stephen: you're not that good. Not in a bad way just…

STEPHEN thinks this is fair.

Love though, fucking hell.

Feel it, every day, I'm filling up with it. Like, I dunno. Something.

She talks to her tummy.

Good job really. Cos you don't stand much of a chance, do you? I am going to have to be pretty on it. No matter. I will be.

D'you want to see?

STEPHEN. Um…?

KAYLEIGH. The scan. They give you a picture. It's actually minging but. Like you can't see anything but.

KAYLEIGH shows STEPHEN the photo.

It's all good. They said that.

Brought it round when I got it but. It was when Winnie was leaving and that so I just. I dunno.

STEPHEN. Oh.

STEPHEN looks at the photo.

He smiles.

KAYLEIGH. You normally, they make you buy it normally, the little picture, but she gave me that one for free. The nurse. Said it'll help me get my head round it. Get bonding and that.

STEPHEN gives the photo back.

It's working.

Keep thinking, can't stop thinking about all the stuff I'll, all the stuff we'll do together. Teach it all the songs my mum taught me, fill its head with them, all centuries of troubles

and struggles and not-to-worrys, so when it's stuck for what
to say or think or do or, or feel there'll just be these little bits
of music, little ribbons, half-remembered, in its head, won't
know why. When it can't find the words it can just.
Hopefully anyway just, sing or whatever.

Cos my mum never shut up with bloody, folk songs.
Hundreds of them. Literally.

STEPHEN. Like what?

KAYLEIGH. Just the old ones, really. Like what we do. Tunes
as well.

STEPHEN. Oh.

KAYLEIGH. That's how they met, her and my dad. At an actual
ceilidh. Just sort of got together for a night or whatever and
then nothing, and then for some naff reason when I was born
she was like: I know what I'll call her.

Think maybe you make quite odd decisions when you've
just given birth. I'm giving my one a couple of days before I
do anything rash.

STEPHEN. Sounds wise.

KAYLEIGH. Thought if it's a girl I might call her Winnie but
then I looked up St Winifred just to see, turns out she was
like this mad Welsh nun who got her head chopped off and
then carried on living. I'm not sure that's what you want for
your daughter. Or it might be a lad, anyway.

So did you?

STEPHEN. Did I…?

KAYLEIGH. Love her? Winnie?

STEPHEN. She was my best friend.

KAYLEIGH. I mean did you fancy her? Like secretly?

STEPHEN. Oh. Um.

STEPHEN *shakes his head*.

KAYLEIGH. Cos she was a nun?

STEPHEN. No. Well. Sort of.

KAYLEIGH. No well sort of.

STEPHEN. I didn't fancy her cos, cos I didn't.

KAYLEIGH. Right.

STEPHEN. I don't, well, hardly fancy anyone really.

And then, the ones I do…

I just like men really. Just, you know…

STEPHEN *searches for the word.*

Men.

KAYLEIGH. Fucking hell, Stephen.

STEPHEN. What?

KAYLEIGH. Nowt just. I dunno. You never said.

STEPHEN. No. No I've, I've not said.

Before now, I mean.

KAYLEIGH. What?

STEPHEN. It just, it was never, so. Couldn't really, well, not with Sister. And anyway it's… I mean, I'll hardly, hardly off to, now it's, by the by really. I just, you, you asked so… Well. That's that.

KAYLEIGH *gets out her phone.*

She takes a picture of STEPHEN.

What are you doing?

KAYLEIGH. Nothing, ignore it.

STEPHEN. What?

KAYLEIGH. Just thought like, probably wouldn't do any harm to just sort of pop you on Grindr, just on my phone.

STEPHEN. I don't understand.

KAYLEIGH. Oh, it's like an app. For hook-ups. It's well famous.

STEPHEN. I still don't understand.

KAYLEIGH. You just put a photo on, like a photo of you or, or sort of probably a photo of your torso, really –

STEPHEN. My torso?

KAYLEIGH. And then other people do, and you can see who's about. See who's nearby. In terms of like other men, in the local area.

STEPHEN. No.

KAYLEIGH. It's fine.

STEPHEN. Kayleigh, no. Stop it. That's not –

KAYLEIGH. Maybe Tinder then?

STEPHEN. What?

KAYLEIGH. It's better cos you only have to talk to people if you both like each other, it's like a swipe thing. Also, no dick pics.

STEPHEN. I don't want to do sort of, anything like that.

KAYLEIGH. It's how you meet someone, Stephen.

It's a good thing.

STEPHEN. No.

KAYLEIGH. Not tonight. Fair enough.

A moment.

STEPHEN. Not sure I'd have many takers anyway.

KAYLEIGH. Fuck off, Stephen, you're a catch.

STEPHEN. Well.

KAYLEIGH. I think so.

If I was a middle-aged gay man from East Yorkshire.

STEPHEN. Right.

KAYLEIGH. Right.

A moment.

I promise I won't put you on Grindr on my phone.

STEPHEN. Right.

KAYLEIGH. It was, you know. Joke.

STEPHEN. Oh. Okay.

STEPHEN *looks at the two pints of Guinness*.

KAYLEIGH. It must be very hard.

Like she was here, and then she just wasn't.

Just happens like that, I think. Sometimes.

STEPHEN *nods*.

He doesn't want to talk about it.

We'd make a good folk song, you know.

STEPHEN. D'you think?

KAYLEIGH. One day.

STEPHEN *smiles*.

STEPHEN. We'd have a lot of verses.

KAYLEIGH. Hopefully.

A moment.

STEPHEN *takes a deep breath*.

STEPHEN. You can, there's a spare room. I've got a. You can
stay with me. And my dad, of course. If that's something, if
that'd be…

KAYLEIGH. Stephen.

STEPHEN. Just while you get sorted out. Or, or till you and
Trev are speaking again.

KAYLEIGH. I'm fine here.

STEPHEN. Not sure you are, Kayleigh.

A moment.

And I'm, well. Be nice. Some company. While I get a bit
more, get started. Job hunt and that.

Might have to get a, computer.

KAYLEIGH. Shit.

STEPHEN. Might need some, well, I mean I will need some, need some help. So it'd be, I'd like it if you… Just for a bit, while you're, we're both getting a bit more, bit more sorted.

KAYLEIGH. Think your dad might find it a bit weird.

STEPHEN. What d'you mean?

KAYLEIGH. I mean, if you just like turn up on the doorstep with a pregnant fifteen-year-old, out of nowhere, I think he might find that a bit weird.

STEPHEN. Maybe, I can, I'll explain. Stuff.

Better than here, Kayleigh. It is.

KAYLEIGH *looks at* STEPHEN.

KAYLEIGH. Are you sure?

STEPHEN *smiles*.

STEPHEN. You should, get your, your things.

KAYLEIGH *goes upstairs*.

STEPHEN *looks around*.

He sits down.

He picks up his low whistle and plays 'Winnie's Slow Air'.

KAYLEIGH *arrives with her bag*.

She sits down.

She listens.

She takes out her whistle.

She adds little moments.

The End.

Also by Tom Wells

JUMPERS FOR GOALPOSTS

THE KITCHEN SINK
and SPACEWANG

ME, AS A PENGUIN,
ABOUT A GOTH
and NOTES FOR FIRST TIME ASTRONAUTS

*Published in print and ebook,
and licensed for amateur performance
by Nick Hern Books*

Other Titles in this Series

A Nick Hern Book

Folk first published as a paperback original in Great Britain in 2016 by Nick Hern Books Limited, The Glasshouse, 49a Goldhawk Road, London W12 8QP, in association with Birmingham Repertory Theatre, Hull Truck Theatre, and Watford Palace Theatre

Folk copyright © 2016 Tom Wells

Tom Wells has asserted his right to be identified as the author of this work

Cover photograph by Graeme Braidwood

Designed and typeset by Nick Hern Books, London
Printed in the UK by Mimeo Ltd, Huntingdon, Cambridgeshire PE29 6XX

A CIP catalogue record for this book is available from the British Library

ISBN   978 1 84842 571 2

www.nickhernbooks.co.uk

facebook.com/nickhernbooks

twitter.com/nickhernbooks